TINY to TODDLER ADVENTURES

with HAVANA

Written by

HAVANA LINDO

Havana Books

New Rochelle, New York

DEDICATION

This book is a dedication to all parents to show how making memories with your children while they are growing up is extremely important. Also, it will show you the importance of investing in your children's futures and allowing them to follow their dreams and aspirations.

October – Month 1
Havana turned 1 month, and she got signed
to a modeling agency and did her 1st paid
photoshoot. She took her 1st passport picture
and celebrated her 1st Halloween.

November – Month 2

Havana turned 2 months and she tried to sit up. She celebrated her 1st Thanksgiving. She also received her 1st passport.

December – Month 3

Havana turned 3 months, got paid for her 2nd commercial for Enfamil, and had a photoshoot for Target. She celebrated her 1st Christmas and took pictures with Santa Claus.

January - Month 4

Havana turned 4 months and she celebrated her 1st New Year. She went to her 1st swimming lesson and took her 1st plane ride to Kingston Jamaica. Havana tasted watermelon and pineapple, got into a hot tub, and visited Dunns River Falls for the 1st time.

my 1ST
Valentine's
Day

February – Month 5

Havana turned 5 months and she celebrated her 1st Valentine's Day. She got Christened in Baltimore, Maryland by Pastor Murray and took her 2nd plane ride to Miami, Florida where she went to the beach for the 1st time.

March- Month 6

Havana turned 6 months and she celebrated her 1st St. Patrick's Day. She crawled on one leg and started to eat baby food.

HAPPY
EASTER

April - Month 7

Havana turned 7 months and she celebrated her 1st Easter. She took pictures with the Easter Bunny
and had her 3rd plane ride to Ocho Rios Jamaica.

May – Month 8

Havana turned 8 months and she started to stand and hold onto furniture around the house. She got paid for her 2nd Ad on Baby List.

June – Month 9

Havana turned 9 months and she took her 4th plane ride to St. Anns, Jamaica. She went on a boat for the 1st time to visit Pelican Bar in St. Elizabeth. Then she went to St. Thomas to experience a mineral bath. While in Jamaica, Havana also tried mango for the 1st time, and she started to make steps.

July – Month 10

Havana turned 10 months and she celebrated her 1st July 4th. She did her 3rd photoshoot and went to Governor's Island in NYC where she took the ferry for the 1st time. She also started to walk.

August - Month 11
Havana turned 11 months and she went to the zoo for the 1st time. Havana went to the Barbie Malibu Cafe in NYC.
Malibu Barbie Café

Happy Birthday
Ha...

September - Month 12

Havana turned 1 year old, and she took her 5th plane ride to Paris, France. She went inside the Eiffel Tower for lunch at Madame Brasserie. Then, Havana went on a kid's Miraculous Cruise and celebrated her birthday at Disneyland Paris. When Havana returned home, she had 2 birthday cakes and got a pink car and bike for her birthday gifts. A few days later, Havana took her 6th plane ride to Aruba where she saw Flamingoes and played in the pool at the water park at De Palm Island.

Meet the Author

Havana is an energetic one-year-old who loves to eat and play. Havana is a smart baby that meets her milestones. Everyone jokingly says Havana lives a soft life. Havana travels and visits many child-friendly places to create memories.